DOROTHY RILEY, a grandchild of George and the middle child of Ilbert and Vera, was born in Bramley. She attended Bramley National School until the age of thirteen, then after a commercial course worked in a Leeds office. Whilst working a forty-five hour week, with leisure time heavily committed to Girl Guides and church organisations, she took the School Certificate externally, without tuition. This opened the way to a teacher training course and at the age of twenty she began forty years of teaching, the last fourteen years as headteacher of a comprehensive school in Pudsey. All academic qualifications – BD, M.Ed., Dip. Theol., ACP – were taken externally, without tuition, whilst working full-time.

Interests, in addition to various roles in Bramley St Peter's Church, have included Bramley Ladies' Choir, classical music, languages and fell-walking.

Dorothy left Bramley in 1990 and now lives in Morecambe and the Isle of Man.

GEORGE'S FAMILY

Scenes from a Past Age

GEORGE'S FAMILY

Scenes from a Past Age

Dorothy Riley

ATHENA PRESS
LONDON

GEORGE'S FAMILY
Scenes from a Past Age
Copyright © Dorothy Riley 2005

All Rights Reserved

No part of this book may be reproduced in any form
by photocopying or by any electronic or mechanical means,
including information storage and retrieval systems,
without permission in writing from both the copyright
owner and the publisher of this book.

ISBN 1 84401 510 6

First Published 2005 by
ATHENA PRESS
Queen's House, 2 Holly Road
Twickenham TW1 4EG
United Kingdom

Printed for Athena Press

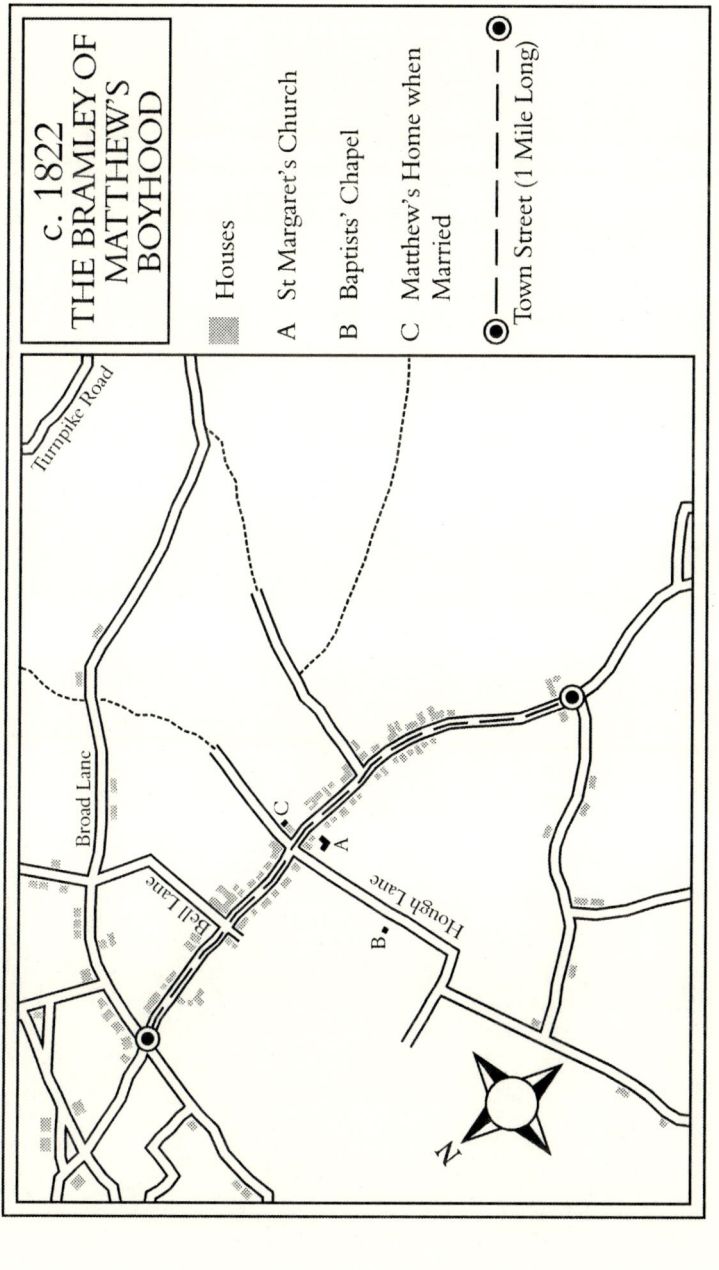

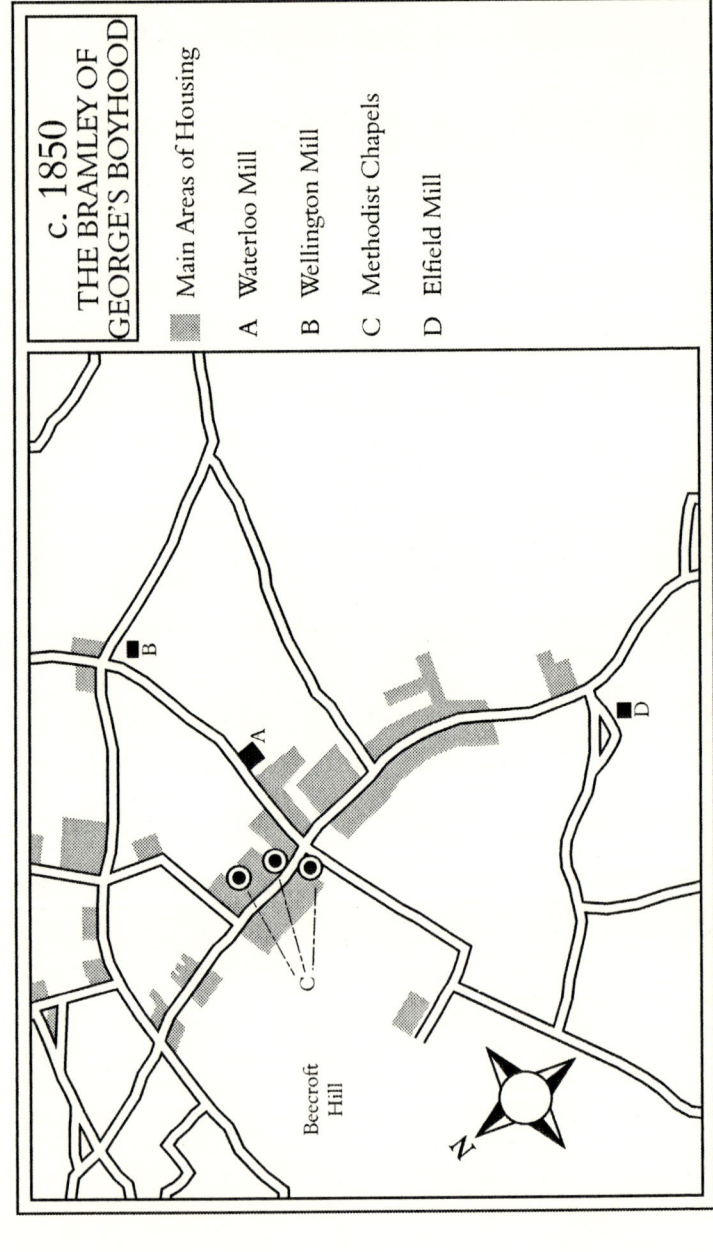

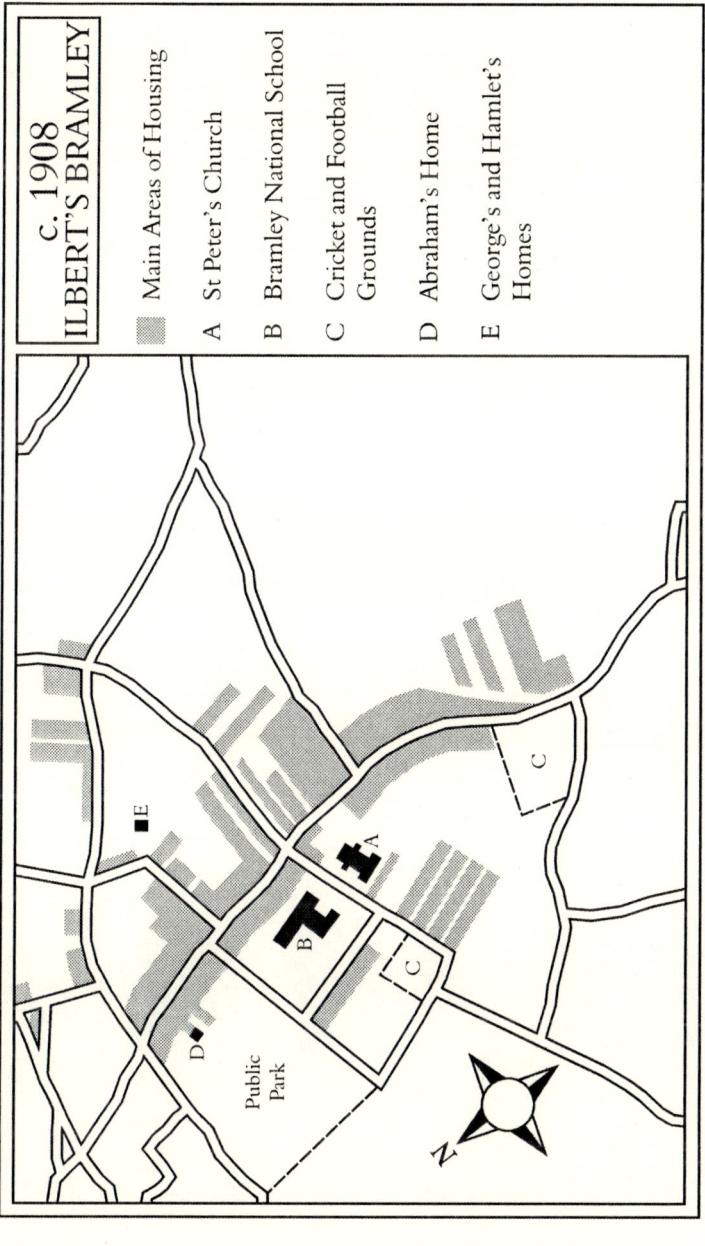

CONTENTS

Introduction	15
An Address to Bramley	17
Prologue	18
Bramley	19
Forefathers	24
Matthew	26
Bramley Band	30
The Bramla Band	34
George's Brothers and Sisters	37
Sarah and Thomas	37
Abraham	37
Jane and Emily (Amelia)	40
Hamlet	40
Hamlet's Children	42
George	45
George's Children	55
The Daughters	55
JANE	55
EDITH	55
MAUDE AND LILLIE	57
ETHEL	62

KATE	62
The Sons	64
LOUIS	64
FRED	65
ILBERT	66
GALEN	73
An Ode to Bramley Town Street	76
Epilogue	78

LIST OF PHOTOGRAPHS

ST MARGARET'S CHAPEL from Town Street	20
STOCKS HILL from an early eighteenth century engraving	21
BRAMLEY OLD CHURCH (ST MARGARET'S CHAPEL) from the south-west	28
BRAMLEY TOWN BAND	32
FAMILY GROUP AT 9 BELL MOUNT	46
GEORGE	47
ST PETER'S CHURCH from the south	48
ST PETER'S CHURCH from the north-west	49
DIETARY TABLE	51
FOUR SISTERS	56
TYPICAL BRAMLEY LADIES	58
ETHEL	61
WEDDING GROUP – Kate's elder daughter	62
ILBERT, c. 1920	67
ILBERT, c. 1904	69
ILBERT AND VERA'S WEDDING, 1922	70

INTRODUCTION

In putting together items of anecdotal family history for the benefit of late-twentieth century members of this Riley family, it became obvious that much of the material could be of interest to a wider range of people who had never heard of George's family: the Rileys of Bramley. But since few people would have heard of this particular Bramley, much less any Rileys who had lived there, would there be any value in publishing very minor and local events?

Many social histories and biographies deal with aspects of life in various centuries and often tend to generalise about living conditions in recording big events and important people. When scientific, technical, political, and social advances cause changes to come about so quickly; when globalisation, travel, and multinational-everything make the world seem smaller; when little seems to be permanent, then ordinary individual, day-to-day lives can easily be forgotten or ignored against the larger picture. Yet such ordinary, individuals are the very essence of civilisation, the raison d'être of governments, social structures, movements, manufacture and trade. Therefore it is appropriate, and not only that but necessary, to show how a few ordinary individuals in one particular place made their contribution to the complex pattern of life in different generations. There was poverty and hardship, deprivation by modern Western standards and a very circumscribed view of the outside world, but there was also courage, loyalty, ideals, philanthropy, and much more of great value.

Almost the whole of what is written here is derived from

word of mouth accounts handed down within the family. In order to preserve something of the anecdotal style little effort has been made to give dates of births, marriages and deaths except where there may be a bearing on the incident recorded or to facilitate linking up with outside events. It will be obvious that very little is recorded about wives and mothers: although – or perhaps, because – they were loved and deeply respected they were not the subject of family anecdotes.

When supplementary background material was necessary it has been mainly drawn, but freely adapted, from the work done by senior boys of Bramley National School (including a Riley!) under the guidance of their teacher Mr ET Carr: *Industry in Bramley* and *The Lands of Bram*.

Accuracy in every detail cannot be fully guaranteed! Care has been taken to give factual information correctly, but many family stories are dependent upon the narrator's memory and any propensity to exaggerate or embellish. Nevertheless it is hoped that the reader will find the accounts both informative and entertaining.

D Riley
2005

AN ADDRESS TO BRAMLEY

Dear village that I love so well,
Fain would I now thy beauties tell,
In words so plain, that all who read
May love thee too in word and deed.
When first the Briton built his hut,
And made thy woods his hunting ground
He never thought this very spot
Would be with such a village crowned.

And as I view thy 'Cottage Homes',
From top of 'Beecroft Hill',
My wayward fancy often roams
To grassy slope and rippling rill,
All decked with fern and bramble fair
With daisies white and poppies red,
Just like an eastern carpet rare,
Around with rich profusion spread.

And now the lark, on pinion strong,
Is carolling his morning lay,
And while I listen to his song
To me the echo seems to say,
'Sweet village that I love so well,
My heart strings are round thee twined,
For in thy name I love to tell,
My home and birthplace are combined.'

Abraham Riley

PROLOGUE

Elizabeth, who was aged about seventy and had been twice married and twice widowed, was paying for her newspapers in the local shop. This meant, of course, having a good gossip with the fairly elderly shopkeeper. In the course of this Elizabeth mentioned her first married name. 'Oh,' said the shopkeeper. 'Are you one of the S... of Kirkstall?'

'No,' replied Elizabeth firmly. 'I am one of the Rileys of Bramley.'

Interesting! Elizabeth's maiden name was indeed Riley, but she had never lived in Bramley. She did, however, remember that at the age of five she had been taken to Bramley by her father, and there she had met Uncle George (actually her father's uncle) and also two of the Miss Rileys. This occasion stayed in her mind as a very important event in her life. To her, the Rileys of Bramley were people of consequence and she 'belonged' with them. The place and the people were inseparable and equally impressive. Why?

BRAMLEY

What there is of the history of this Bramley has been recorded by others, but the scanty records of earlier times in Bramley are not easily obtainable and the 'village' itself is now known only as a suburb of Leeds. A little background information will, therefore, be helpful in understanding the feelings George's family had for their village.

Bramley occupies a ridge on the south side of the Aire valley midway between Leeds and Bradford, rising to about four hundred feet above sea level. The name is Anglo-Saxon and probably means, 'the place of brambles' or maybe 'the field of Bram'. Whatever the meaning of the name, in pre-Norman conquest times the land belonged to an Anglo-Saxon named Archil and was inhabited by about ten families, numbering perhaps forty people. The *Doomsday Book* shows that at that time there were 600 acres of agricultural land and only a handful of villagers. William the Conqueror gave the whole of this area to Ilbert de Laci. Little changed for centuries: more cultivated land, more villagers, and a gradual growth of the necessary crafts and occupations to sustain village life.

From the wooded slope on the north side of the village the inhabitants could look down on Kirkstall Abbey and its surrounding fields and across the River Aire to the lightly populated other side of the dale. Four miles or so to the east there was the township of Leeds; to the south and west, open undulating lower Pennine countryside with a number of small villages. The main trading routes did not go through Bramley except for touching the borders to avoid the difficult terrain near the river and various small becks.

This was, in those earlier centuries, an area very little

troubled by what went on in the world at large, where people were able, on the whole, to support themselves but had to work hard to do so and had little to spare. The population increased slowly. By the middle of the seventeenth century there seems to have been about 350 inhabitants, of whom only fifty-six households were liable to pay the 1663 Hearth Tax. The number of inhabitants had risen to about 450 by the beginning of the eighteenth century.

ST MARGARET'S CHAPEL from Town Street.

In all these earlier centuries the religious life of the Bramley community was not much in evidence. When the parochial system was established in the area (circa 1100) Bramley was included in the parish of Leeds, and baptisms, weddings, and burials were performed there. Records of such events are missing or incomplete. It is doubtful if many villagers attended a church service more than once a year. Wandering Presbyterian preachers found fruitful ground at Bramley, and baptisms were sometimes performed in private houses without being officially recorded. In 1731 a church dedicated to St Margaret was erected in the centre of the village, and a little later the Methodists and Baptists also had chapels. In 1863 St Margaret's was replaced by an entirely new building dedicated to St Peter.

The main thoroughfare was, and still is, the one-mile long Town Street. Near the halfway point was the town well at Stocks Hill, and although it was rumoured that the graveyard drained into the spring feeding the town well this was never proved.

STOCKS HILL from an early eighteenth century engraving. The town well is in the foreground.

Most of the housing was on or just off Town Street and all the cottages and houses were built of local stone from

Bramley Fall quarry until near the end of the nineteenth century. A particular feature was the considerable number of small yards just off the main street with little two or even three one-room storeys on each side of the yard with the master's larger house at the far end. These were both the living accommodation and the work places of the majority of Bramley inhabitants: the family lived on the ground floor with hand-loom weaving or other crafts being carried on in the upper room(s). Often the owners of the cottages had a small piece of land nearby which served either as a place to stretch the woollen cloth on tenters, or to keep one or two animals.

There was no piped water supply and no sewage system until late in the nineteenth century. Night soil was put on a dung heap in the middle of the yard, sometimes only a few feet from the cottages. One traditional story, passed down in several families, states that a donkey stumbled into one of these dung heaps and was suffocated. A water cart came round each day to collect the night slops, the urine was taken for use in the dyeing process. Unsurprisingly, cholera outbreaks occurred from time to time. A particularly severe one came in 1811 when over 200 locals died.

Education in the sense of formal schooling hardly existed. In the eighteenth century there were a few, very few, private schools for the children of the small number of villagers who could afford to pay. The only available source of education for other children was provided after 1754 in a school attached to the church – but some payment was required – or at Sunday schools and night schools where basic reading and writing were taught. It is therefore not surprising that in his *History of the West Riding* written in 1834, Edward Parsons wrote of the Bramley area:

> It is generally stated that the inhabitants of these busy scenes of industry are rude to fierceness in their

deportment, and that they are lost in ignorance upon every topic which is not involved in their manual occupation. This is only partially correct. In these villages there are many truly respectable individuals and families, whose manners, without partaking of the affected refinement far too common in our large towns, are highly agreeable, whose information is as extensive as reading and thought can make it, whose rural principle attaches a sterling weight to their character, and whose spirit of charity, benevolence and patriotism attaches honour to their names. Of rudeness and ignorance there is indeed enough, but these are not so common as they were a few years ago.

It is with this background in mind that George's family can be appreciated.

FOREFATHERS

Little clear information is available as to when the Rileys first lived in Bramley. The name Riley, which comes from 'stream' and 'field', is common in Pennine districts and there were Rileys in and around the Leeds area from the Middle Ages onwards. As has already been noted, parish and other records in earlier centuries were often missing or incomplete. Births, marriages and deaths which should have been recorded at Leeds parish church were frequently not recorded at all. Occasionally, especially after the Commonwealth period, a few, but very few, marriages and burials were recorded as having taken place in Bramley itself.

By the eighteenth century there certainly were several Riley households in Bramley. William Ryly/Riley (both spellings are found) was born in 1719 and died in 1794; Samuel Riley lived at the same time and was also long-lived for those times. Both of these men had a number of children, both had a son named John and each John had a son or grandson named Joseph. Nothing is known about their occupations. There was also a Matthew Riley – no details – and a Martin Riley, described on his daughter's baptismal entry in 1831 as a clothier. One Joseph, not necessarily either of the two already mentioned, married to Alice, was also described as a clothier, but also, at the baptism of another child, as a farmer. The baptismal records of the children of one of the John Riley's, with a wife named Jane, describe him as cordwainer and shoemaker. So much work was seasonal, as in agriculture, or variable because of trade fluctuations, that many villagers had at least two occupations.

It is probable that William was the direct ancestor of George's family through his son John to Joseph, George's grandfather. It is certain that none of the earlier Rileys were among the wealthier villagers. The list of residents who had paid the Hearth Tax years before had not contained a Riley – but it is worth noting that of those who had paid the tax, fifty-six on the list, only six could actually sign their names, the others made a cross. Therefore it seems that although the various Rileys had little money they were in most respects no different from the entire population of Bramley at that time. Towards the end of the eighteenth century a William Riley – there was more than one – was provided with a coat from the parish's Poor Relief fund.

Joseph, George's grandfather, was a labourer. This probably means that he did any work that was available without having any special expertise: seasonal agricultural work, quarrying, or jobs in the woollen industry are most likely. All wages were low, so any man employed as a labourer, whether fully employed or casual, would barely earn enough to keep a wife and family. Joseph married Mary and they had children, one was named Joseph and another named Matthew. It was Matthew who was George's father.

MATTHEW

Matthew was born in 1813, when economic conditions in Bramley were still very difficult. All that is known about his early years is that at a very young age he would be working full-time with little opportunity for education.

Weaving was still done in cottages or in weaving rooms belonging to the wealthier 'masters'. Children were employed mainly as scribbler fillers, that is, feeding the dyed loose wool on to the scribbling or carding machine which straightened the wool ready for spinning. Similar non-skilled work could be easily found. The hours were long when business was good. The day usually started at 6 a.m. (or 7 a.m. in winter) and went on well into the evening. At very busy times it was known for work to go on until about 11 p.m. and there were occasions when the children would spend the night sleeping among the looms. As well as the cottage industry there were also some mills, usually for specific parts of the process, such as scribbling. Whether in the cottages or the mills the children would earn about three shillings for a full week's work, which might be up to ninety hours.

Joseph Rogerson who lived in Bramley at about the same time as Matthew, but who was some years older, kept a diary covering the years between 1808 and 1814, often referring to general matters. He wrote of the difficulty of getting an education: when there was plenty of work there was no time for schooling, and when there was no work, there was no money to pay for schooling. Matthew would certainly have been in that situation but equally, like most boys of his age, he would have learned to read and write at Sunday school.

When Matthew was older and stronger he left the weaving industry and began to work as a builder or stonemason, probably through some connection from his father's labouring. At some time, in his young adult years, Matthew was one of a group of men who kept themselves informed about what was happening in the country generally. Cloth and other goods made in Bramley were usually taken into Leeds, and one man who went to Leeds would buy a newspaper and on returning would read it to a group who gathered outside or sometimes inside one of the public houses in the centre of Bramley. The information thus provided was disseminated through the village by word of mouth.

Matthew married twice. First to Lavinia (or Lavena) Bates: the marriage took place in Leeds parish church, or was registered there, but Lavinia had some connection with one of the non-conformist churches. There were two children from this marriage. After Lavinia's death Matthew married again, this time to Mary Haley, a member of another well known Bramley family and they had five children. Their home was a small stone-built cottage in the centre of the village in a recently renamed road, Waterloo Lane.

A capable, enterprising, and energetic man, Matthew had become a skilled stonemason, but with no safety standards of any significance, building was a dangerous occupation. When he was working on the building of a new church, St Matthew's, in Meanwood, he fell from the scaffolding of the building. His injuries were serious: he was unable to work after the fall and died in November 1850 from injuries to his lungs caused by the accident eighteen months earlier, according to his death certificate. This must have been a very difficult time for Mary in particular, with a family of young children. The two older children, Sarah Ann, aged fifteen, and Thomas, fourteen, were already working and the small amount they earned was the family's main income. Jane was six, Abraham five, George three, and Hamlet one. Amelia, also known as Emily, was born just after her father's death.

Here family 'history' and baptism records do not sit easily together. The story is that Matthew and Mary had worshipped in one of the Methodist chapels, but after Matthew's accident when help was really needed, no one from the Methodists offered help or even came to express sympathy. Help was offered by the Vicar and members of the Anglican Church, so Mary therefore decided the family would become Church of England worshippers. Baptismal records show that Jane, Abraham and George were actually baptised before Matthew's accident. However, it was not unusual for children to be baptised in an Anglican church when the family worshiped in a Methodist chapel.

BRAMLEY OLD CHURCH (ST MARGARET'S CHAPEL) from the south-west. The church in which George and his siblings were Baptised.

The headstone on Matthew's grave was of some interest. It was probably erected much later than his death and was no doubt paid for by the family into which Amelia had married, as she was buried in the same grave as Matthew. In any case, Mary would not have had money to spare for a fine gravestone. The inscription began: 'Matthew Riley, builder of this town...' but there were people who objected to this. The protest was that Matthew did not build the town so a comma had to be inserted to make the inscription read: 'Matthew Riley, builder, of this town...' The headstone showed very clearly that the comma had been engraved later than the rest, even after more than a century of being 'weathered'.

Matthew had no real chance of bringing up his family, but in the short time he had and through his wife, he set them on the right path.

BRAMLEY BAND

During Matthew's lifetime Bramley band was formed with Riley involvement from the beginning and for most of its existence, although as far as is known, Matthew himself had no part in it. The band had a number of different names over the years: Bramley Reed Band, Bramley Old Band, Bramley Temperance Band – the first in England it was claimed – Bramley Christian Mission Band, Bramley Brass Band and plain Bramley Band. Many of the bandsmen were the same whatever the title of the band.

The first band was formed in 1828 by a farm man, a member of the Hesling family, and had seven or eight instrumentalists. They practised among the handlooms in the cottage of Mr Hesling's son. By 1831 there were fourteen instrumentalists who were recorded as playing to celebrate the coronation of William IV. Joseph Riley was a trombonist in the early bands, and for years later. This Joseph was probably Matthew's uncle or cousin rather than his father or brother as there are no family stories about him.

Practising, apart from full band practices, was not easy for some because the cottages were so small. One of Joseph's fellow trombonists was a particularly good player, and used to boast that he could do nine feet six inches of slotting in a bar of quick step time. The cottage in which he lived was so small that he could not make his A flat with the door shut, so his slide came out into the street causing no small risk to passers-by.

Many of the band's engagements were for elections

playing for each party as required. One of the early engagements reads:

> NOV. 1ST 1839 PLAYING FOR BRAMLEY YELLOWS, 15/-
>
> NOV. 1ST 1839 PLAYING FOR THE BLUES, £2

There was an additional note:

> The Blues had got some of the Yellow voting papers with the Blue party's name on them, so when the votes were counted the second time the Blues had won.
>
> 1841 Election. Leeds. Yellows, four days, fifteen men, £45 10d

The number of players in the band fluctuated considerably depending upon the employment situation of the time. For a short period in 1846 it had dwindled to three players, one of them being John Riley, a trombone player. He had long service with the band – over fifty years – and was the Membership Secretary for quite a lot of that time. He was 'Bramley' by family and affection, but lived first in Armley then in Stanningley, just outside the Bramley boundary.

Engagements to play came from a wide variety of functions: galas, flower shows, official openings of railway lines and similar services, and, of course, contests. Many of the bandsmen relied on their share of what the band earned to increase their meagre wages. These engagements took place in more distant cities than Leeds, such as Liverpool, Hull, Manchester, Birmingham and London, and the Bramley band could only go because the organisers paid travelling expenses. When the band went to London in 1860 for five days, one bandsman set off with three teacakes and 9d in cash and another took half an ounce of tobacco, 11d and a sandwich. In London, they walked about seven miles to a small boarding house, kept by a Bramley man, where there was only room to sleep on the floor downstairs as there were already sixty people sleeping in the bedrooms.

In 1871 they were engaged to play as the band of the Prince of Wales Own Yorkshire Hussars at York for a fortnight. They had to wear uniforms and mount horses, but most of them being hand-weavers, had never been on a horse before and had to be propped up on their horses until they moved forward to play. One by one, they were thrown from the horses, and one man was rescued from under the horse, clinging grimly to the saddle which had slipped round. Another, as told in the poem 'Bramla Band' ended up in the big drum. Lord Wenlock asked this man if he was hurt, then said 'Where is your horse, my man?' to get the reply 'In hell, I hope, my Lord.'

BRAMLEY TOWN BAND, Bramley Carnival, May 3 1913.

They were very successful in competitions throughout most of the existence of the band. One example was a contest at Crystal Palace, London, in 1904 where they were awarded the second prize in the Preliminary Shield Contest against twenty other bands. Only second prize, but the secretary of the contest was so impressed that he wrote a letter of congratulation and at his own expense had their certificate framed and stamped in gold letters, saying that their performance was, in his opinion, equivalent to winning several first prizes in the general run of contests.

One of the low points, perhaps the lowest, was not referred to in the 'official' history of the band. At one contest a large entry had been expected so there were seven prizes, but only six bands turned up. Sadly, Bramley Band was only awarded the *seventh* prize.

Over the years, the band won nearly one hundred cups, shields and other prizes in addition to sixty-three gold and silver medals. They played before Queen Victoria and the Prince Consort at Lancaster Castle.

THE BRAMLA BAND

Who hesn't heerd o' t'Bramla Band
That's famous far an' near?
An' wins sich honor for aar taan,
Wi' ivvery cumin' year.
At Gala, Feast an' Flaar-shew,
At Kirsmas an' May-day,
At Contest tew, aar Band is suar
To carry t'prize away.

Wi' bran new clothes an' instruments
All shinin' bright and clear, -
An' lads an' lasses craadin' round,
The big drum in the rear, –
The men all marchin' breast to breast,
Wi' martial stride and pomp, –
Who can withstand their stirring strains
As daan the taan they tromp.

Nah, whether t'band chaps play'd ta mitch
(For t'trumpets didn't rust.)
I cannot say, but suar enif
They blew 'em 'til they brust.
T'poor chaps were omast fit to roar,
For all thur brass wor spent,
But t'taan clubbed up, and bowt each man
A grand new instrument.

Sum wor silver, and sum wor brass,
An' nicely curled i' t'middle, –
An' sum they went – trom, trom! Bom, bom!

An' sum did nowt but twiddle –
An' sum hed keys, an' hoils, an' lids,
An' wun, a queer consarn,
Had nyther keys, nor hoils, nor lid,
But slotted up an' daan.

But when they played 'em all at wunce,
An' mixt 'em weel together,
An' when the chap upon t'big drum,
Thum, thum! Began to leather,
T'effect wor really killin',
An' a captain from the wars
Enlisted 'em for sodgers, in
The 'Prince of Wales Huzzars'.

Nah, sum hed nivver ridden a horse,
Except at Bramla Tide, –
An' then upon the willy-gigs
Sometimes they'd had a ride.
So, when ther regimentals com,
An' they began to don,
They couldn't tell what t'spurs wor for,
Unless to hod 'em on.

They thowt if they were fastened tight,
Ta t'horse they'd sum hah stick –
An' then they couldn't be thrown off
If t' horse began to kick.
So off they went full trot to York,
Though nearly jost to jelly; –
They stuck ta t'pummel, an' kep ther spurs
Weel under t'horse's belly.

An' when they gat ta t'city walls,
They pool'd up in a raw,

An' 'See the Conquering Hero comes',
They all began to blaw.
An' varry weel they played it tew,
When t'horses didn't prance,
But when they hurd a lively bit,
They seemed abaat to dance.

At last that chap wi' t'slotting thing,
Wi' cheeks puff'd fit to crack,
He thrust it aat sa varry far
He cuddn't pool it back –
An' t'horse being rayther freeten'd tew,
An' feelin' summat prickin',
It started off a-raumin' up,
An' then began a-kickin'.

First, t'instrument flew on to t'ground,
An' jingald fit to breck,
Then he wor fetched all on a lump,
Reight on to t'horse's neck,
But t'warst of all a spur cam off,
An' t'chap being aat of plumb,
T'horse sent him flyin' like a shot
Heeard first into t'big drum.

They pool'd him att bi his coit tail,
An' sum began to chaff,
But t'chap wor suar he'd neer been thrawn
If t'spur hed not come off.
So, readers, nivver use a thing
Ye dunnot understand,
An' if yer tempted so to dew,
Remember t'Bramla Band.

John T Barker: member of an old Bramley family.

GEORGE'S BROTHERS AND SISTERS

Sarah and Thomas

Both these older children of Matthew and Mary were working for some years before their father's death. The work was the usual kind for Bramley children, but by this time there was little left of the cottage woollen industry and most of the work was done in the dozen or so mills which had been built at various times.

Sarah was for some time, at least until her mid-teens, a scribbler filler, but later went into service with the family of one of the quarry owners or stone merchants. There was no family reference to her after this point.

Thomas may or may not have left mill work but he eventually left Bramley although only as far as one of the neighbouring 'townships'. He had a fairly large family, and one of his sons was named Matthew – the father of the Elizabeth mentioned in the Prologue.

Abraham

Like the rest of Matthew's children, Abraham started work as soon as he was old enough. He and his brothers and sisters were, however, given the opportunity to attend school: a small payment was charged according to the lessons provided; for example, Reading and Writing 3d a week, History and Geography 4d, Mapping and Drawing 6d and so on, but there were a number of free places. Probably the help given to the family by the Vicar was to enable them to have free places. Even so, working life began very young. At the age of eight they were working part-time and began full-time work not long afterwards.

The only family story to come from this period suggests Abraham's potential as a businessman. Being the eldest of the three and more experienced, he was entrusted with their dinner money – a good filling dinner could be bought for very few pence. Abraham convinced George and Hamlet that too much meat would overheat their blood and be bad for them while to have only vegetables would be very healthy. Of course, just vegetables cost only a small fraction of the price of the full meal, and Abraham secretly kept the rest of the money. This worked until their mother wondered why they were so hungry day after day and asked what they had eaten for dinner! Needless to say, Abraham was firmly dealt with, and his money-making scheme ended.

In spite of this lapse, Abraham was an intelligent and hard-working boy. He left mill work and gained employment in a local shop, able before long to set up business himself as a grocer.

In 1865 at the age of twenty-one Abraham married Sarah Newton, the daughter of an auctioneer and valuer, and Abraham began to interest himself in this new occupation. The couple lived at first in a small house on Town Street, but later moved to a 'better' property. Sarah's father lived in the neighbouring parish of Wortley but owned land in Bramley which he passed to his daughter. At some later stage in their marriage a minor argument led Abraham to say: 'Thee can get out of my house!' to which Sarah replied 'Thee can get thy house off my land!' It is not certain in which of their houses this occurred as they moved again to a house in Moorfields, one of the most select areas.

There were a number of children born to Abraham and

Sarah. The eldest was a boy named Isaac with the additional name Newton. Other children were Walter, Eliza, Bertha Newton and David Carlyle. Isaac became known as the black sheep of the family without elaboration of what he had done to deserve this title. It was not a financial matter, because he continued to work as a clerk in his father's business. By the time that David was born Abraham had become an auctioneer and valuer himself. Eliza had died aged one year; there is no family information about Walter and Bertha. David in due course joined his father in their family business, run from premises from the top of Bell Lane. The business flourished and expanded; they were estate agents as well as auctioneers/valuers with branches in both Bramley and Pudsey.

Abraham did not confine his activity only to business. From early years he had made use of the Mechanics' Institute which had social facilities such as billiards and other sports. More importantly for Abraham it had a good, and for the times, extensive library. There were regular lectures and debates on a very wide range of subjects. It was said that Abraham had taught himself four languages, but it is not known if he ever went abroad. Latin was one of the languages he learnt.

It is not known if he had ever played any instrument, but he was for many years the President of the Bramley Band. Local events, the church and the Conservative Club all received his ready support.

Such a great rise from the poverty of his earlier years is worthy of many anecdotes, but there are none. Perhaps his loyalty in standing beside his 'disgraced' son put a little distance between him and George's family, but they were still very proud of him.

Jane and Emily (Amelia)

It is strange that there were no stories that featured either of the girls, but perhaps the explanation is that they were so much like most of the girls in what they did and what they had to deal with. As family circumstances improved, Jane was able to give more time to helping her mother and then she married a local man and lived quietly in Bramley to a good old age. Emily, referred to mainly by this less formal name, did her share of housekeeping and when Hamlet set up his own home she ran his house until he married and she also married and continued to live in Bramley.

Hamlet

The youngest boy in the family, Hamlet, had a somewhat more retiring character than his brothers but shared most of the same qualities. Being in the background seemed to have started when he was a baby; the 1851 census and the record of his baptism give different dates for his birth – no doubt due to the problems his mother had to cope with at the time. He was particularly close to George, working with him as a boy, then going into the market gardening business as a partner in Riley Bros, then, when setting up his own home, living next door (semi-detached) to George.

Whilst his sister Emily kept house for him he gave a home for an unknown period to a nephew who had the Christian name of Riley. Shortly afterwards, Hamlet married Ellen Dawson, of an old Bramley family, and they had three daughters: Mary, Hilda, and Nellie.

Hamlet had the great virtue of being able to give quiet support and encouragement to others. Not only did he do his full share with George in the demanding market gardening and rhubarb-growing business, but he also took an interest in Abraham's work as an auctioneer and valuer. He was himself interested in art and architecture and with different circumstances in his early years might have developed this interest and taken up an occupation involving something of that kind. In his home Hamlet had pictures and *objets d'art* which were not of much monetary value but were of unusual interest. There is no specific information that he enjoyed travelling, but he did visit the Channel Islands, an unusual destination from Bramley at that period.

HAMLET'S CHILDREN

Of the three daughters born to Hamlet and Ellen, there is little to record about the youngest daughter, Nellie. She was never very robust and lived quietly at home carefully tended by her sisters, who held her in great affection.

Neither Mary nor Hilda married, and they lived together all their lives in the house in which they had grown up, hardly ever leaving Bramley. Like their cousins when the Riley Bros business required extra hands, they gave help. Hilda could actually do little to help because she had a deformed left arm which had never grown to the correct length. The explanation given by Mary and Hilda was that when Hilda was born, the midwife put her down whilst she attended to the mother but had unthinkingly placed her on a marble slab, the coldness thereby causing irreparable harm. They neither sought nor required any other explanation of the deformity.

It is appropriate to give an account of these two sisters together rather than separately as not only were their lives and habits intertwined but also their conversations. Mary might begin:

'We had a visit from – didn't we, Hilda?'

'We did, Mary, we did.'

'And he (or she) said to us… didn't he, Hilda?'

'He did, Mary, he did.'

'He actually said… didn't he, Hilda?'

And so on, taking ten minutes to report a two-minute conversation. Occasionally Hilda would introduce this kind of conversation, but usually Mary was the leader. They must have spent many hours going over the conversations they had had with their very rare visitors or even with their local tradesmen.

On one occasion the Vicar called on them and said 'I thought it must be some time since I visited the Miss Rileys.'

'Yes, Vicar,' said Mary promptly. 'It will be two years and a fortnight come Friday since your last visit. We were boiling some onions and you said that you liked boiled onions.'

The Vicar felt compelled to assure them that there would not be such a long interval before his next visit.

Another feature of their conversations was one often found in small communities: they loved recounting the relationship between one person and another or just to give the family background of a person who had been mentioned: 'Now she was the daughter of … who was the cousin of … and his second cousin married … who…' and so on. But they managed not to lose the thread of the story they were telling.

Despite their very secluded lives Mary and Hilda were convinced that being one of the Bramley Rileys was to be a person of importance. Making a very rare journey into Leeds, Mary went into one of the major department stores to buy some dress material. Almost every dress, blouse, skirt, or coat that both Mary and Hilda wore was scarcely distinguishable from every other dress, blouse, skirt, or coat they had ever had – navy blue with a pattern of small flowers and just plain navy or black for the skirts and coats. Yet buying new material was still a very weighty matter. Mary went to the fabric department, seated herself on a chair and demanded to see the manager, who, she said, always attended to her. When the manager of the department came, Mary announced 'I am Miss Riley of Bramley, and I always get my material here. Bring me…

such and such.' The bemused manager, who had probably hardly heard of Bramley and never of a Miss Riley of Bramley, would obediently provide all her simple requirements.

In similar vein, there was the occasion when they saw in the newspaper a notice about a large Leeds store promoting the sale of boiled ham, and perhaps with the sale of whole hams in mind, the store promised same-day delivery. Mary and Hilda who had no telephone, by some means found someone to get a message to the store: a quarter of a pound of boiled ham to be delivered to their home that same day. It came.

They were 'characters', and would have been so in any period. What had been good enough for dear father was good enough for them, in religion, politics and social customs. But they were kindly ladies who looked for the best in other people and would not have anything to do with malicious or unsavoury gossip. They were appreciative of anything done for them. They expressed their opinions openly, took a lively interest in the people they knew, and took pleasure and pride in their family connections.

GEORGE

George, born in 1846, never really knew his father, Matthew, as a strong and vigorous man, and in fact had little direct knowledge of him at all. His elder brother Abraham was his guiding light at first. George would not, however, meekly follow Abraham: he was every bit as able and enterprising and developed his own interests and way of life.

Bramley was in the great West Riding rhubarb-growing triangle, and trade in rhubarb really flourished in the second half of the nineteenth century. George was quick to see the possibilities for a profitable occupation, with general market gardening alongside to fill the quiet months. He and his younger brother rented or bought suitable fields of various sizes from about one acre to thirteen acres. Some, not all, of these fields had forcing sheds – only forced rhubarb had any sale value. In autumn the rhubarb roots were put into the totally dark sheds which were heated by a system of flue pipes from a coke fire. The rhubarb sticks would be ready for picking by late December or early January, picked by candlelight as anything stronger would spoil the delicate colouring of the pink sticks with the pure yellow leaf top. The sticks were immediately bound in half pound bundles and packed carefully in boxes to be sent by rail to various city wholesalers. It was intensive work at this time and also in spring when the sheds were emptied and the fields prepared for the next season. Other vegetable crops in the main summer and autumn business were usually sold fairly locally.

At the age of twenty-two George married Elizabeth Turner and they lived in Bell Lane. His mother, Mary, lived with them until her death in 1881. They moved after her death and lived for many years in Bell Mount, unusual in being brick-built. The house had two ground floor rooms and a cellar, two main bedrooms and a half-size one, and an attic room, also used as a bedroom. There was no bathroom and the WC, as for most housing then, was outside. George and Elizabeth had ten children, and this house could only provide enough accommodation for the family because the older children were married and living elsewhere before the younger ones needed more space. The children were: Jane, Edith, Louis, Maude, Lillie, Ethel, Fred, Kate, Ilbert, and Galen.

FAMILY GROUP AT 9 BELL MOUNT. Hamlet's house is the adjoining semi.

As rhubarb growing was only labour-intensive for part of the year, workers were only employed on a temporary or casual basis and, additionally, the whole family when old enough – including the girls – were drafted in to do much of the work. George's children did however all go to school up to the age of twelve or so, Bramley National School having been established in 1850, and George encouraged all his children to take advantage of and participate in everything that was available in both study and sport. Swimming was a particular interest: George was President of Bramley Swimming Club for over twenty years and both Ilbert and Galen gained Royal Lifesaving Society Bronze awards, and George also presented a shield for annual swimming competitions among the Bramley schools.

Presented to
MR GEO. RILEY F.R.M.S.
BY THE MEMBERS OF THE BRAMLEY & DISTRICT GENTS SWIMMING CLUB,
AS A MARK OF RESPECT & ESTEEM ON THE OCCASION OF HIS 21ST YEAR
AS PRESIDENT 1925.

GEORGE

George certainly required his children to be well-behaved at home and in public. When they were going to any social event or party, he would line up the younger children and give them each one stroke of the cane or strap to remind them what would happen if they misbehaved. At home, he believed that keeping the children busy was the best way to ensure good behaviour.

George kept himself busy. In addition to his market gardening he was able to devote a lot of time to his other main interest – the 'villagers' of Bramley. Local politics, the parish church, sport and education, local events, and charitable work all benefited from his participation spread over many years. Standing as a Conservative, he became a councillor for the Bramley ward on Leeds City Council, mainly so that he could ensure that Bramley was given due attention. He served in this capacity for fifteen years.

ST PETER'S CHURCH from the south, the church in which George's children and grandchildren were Baptised.

As well as attending church regularly with the family, George was a long-serving churchwarden and had contributed generously to the building fund for the new church put up in 1863. The family story is that the Rileys paid for the bells in the new church, but official sources credit two other families with having, between them, provided the bells. As often happens with building funds, items are given estimated costs for fund raising purposes and people are asked to give what seems appropriate with these costs in mind. It is likely that the Rileys gave a sum of money with the cost of the bells merely as a guide.

ST PETER'S CHURCH from the north-west.

His concern for the welfare of the people in the village showed very strongly in the time he devoted to his work as a Guardian. The Bramley (Poor Law) Union was first formed in 1862 and the Guardians were the committee members responsible for the administration of the laws for the relief of the poor, by running the workhouse and dealing with the needs of paupers and vagrants. By the time George became a Guardian the Bramley Union was a ward in a wider group of small townships and Bramley had six Guardians. For many years George was Chairman of the Board of Guardians and therefore ex officio on all the committees. When he was not Chairman he was a member of the Assessment Committee, the Building Committee, the Children's Homes Committee and the Farm Sub-Committee, all at the same time.

Very detailed rules and procedures were laid down for the officers of the workhouse and poor relief. There was a Master of the Workhouse who received free residence and food and was paid (at the beginning of the twentieth century) £70 per annum. The Matron was paid £40 per annum, and the other resident staff received various smaller amounts, such as £30 per annum to the cook, and £12 per annum to the resident barber. Some indication of the responsibility these officers and Guardians had, and the impact on the people of Bramley, is shown by the number needing Poor Relief. For example, in 1901 Bramley had a total adult population of 17,299 and of these over 200 were inmates of the workhouse and over 900 received outdoor relief. These figures did not include vagrants nor those who received only medical relief. The average weekly cost of maintenance for inmates worked out at about 4s 1d per head. Dietary tables were drawn up for every meal on every day of the week, and a footnote stated that only half the allowance of bread should be put out for each meal: if the inmates asked for the full amount it must be given to them, but otherwise it should be kept for the next meal.

DIETARY TABLE. The whole week's diet was set out in this way.

Duties as a Guardian were taken very seriously by George who was in no sense just a committee man concerned with self-aggrandisement. His decisions were made without being influenced by what other people might think of him or his motives.

His genuine interest was shown in other ways too. When extra help for the market garden and rhubarb fields was needed he employed among others, men who needed a fresh start or a helping hand; a young man who had served a

51

sentence in a reformatory; another who had been in prison and a disabled man.

The latter was innocently and unfortunately involved in an incident which caused much amusement among sections of the villagers for some time afterwards – losing nothing in the telling. The man concerned had two wooden legs, peg legs, of the most basic type, not much more than wooden batons. During working hours he went to the WC which was in a very small shed at the edge of the field. He could not shut the door and sat on the toilet with his wooden legs protruding outside. At the same time another casual worker was told to get a wheelbarrow 'from the shed yonder' so hurried off and grasped what he thought were wheelbarrow handles, but instead he pulled his unfortunate co-worker off the toilet! Everyone but the indignant victim found this very funny, the general standard of humour being rather unsophisticated.

A similar unsympathetic sense of humour was shown in another incident known to George, although it did not directly concern his family, workers or property. Just across the road from one of the rhubarb fields some small terraced back-to-back houses had been built. These were always referred to as 'the brick buildings' because all the other houses in that area were older and built of stone. These brick houses had one room downstairs plus a small kitchen, a cellar, and one bedroom upstairs, and some had an attic. Toilets were outside in small blocks between the terraced houses. In each house the staircase led up directly from the outside door. One of these houses was the home of a very fat woman, who when going upstairs, needed to use her hands on the steps (she could not see where her feet were) and she came down the stairs the same way, that is, backwards. Making this difficult journey one day – either up or down it makes no difference – she lost her footing and fell backwards down the stairs. She crashed against the door at the bottom: with the force of the fall and her weight the door shattered and she was tightly wedged amid the wreckage. Hearing footsteps outside she shrieked loudly: 'Fotch a doctor! Fotch a doctor!' The footsteps were those of a passing workman who surveyed the situation then said brightly: 'Nay, Missis, it's noan a doctor tha wants, it's a joiner,' and went happily on his way. Fortunately the woman's neighbours were more helpful.

George probably demanded even more of himself than he did of others; self-reliance, self-control, and using one's abilities to the full were important to him. Even in his busy life he found time for some serious intellectual work, making a very thorough study of the Bramley area, not just of its history but its geology and related sciences. An exercise in self-control is shown in an entirely different context. Before he went on an excursion to the Isle of Man he was told that the best way to avoid seasickness was to look at the horizon and breathe steadily. So for the whole crossing both ways, almost four hours each time, he stood near the ship's bows gazing steadily ahead and breathing deeply. He was not seasick but some others were. No doubt it was not anywhere near a rough crossing or perhaps he was naturally a good sailor, but his determination is still impressive.

Determination can easily become obstinacy, and there were times when George seemed to take pleasure in being obstinate. One such incident was when he turned eighty. He tried to board a tram which had begun to move, missed his step and scraped his shins on the cast-iron footplate. A lady who lived nearby saw him returning home with indications of an accident and as she had been a nurse in the Boer War, she rushed round to give help. She was horrified at the injury to his right leg, bathed it, bandaged it, fussed and lectured non-stop and at some length. When she eventually left, George laughed quite heartily, and said

'Such a fuss! I wonder what she would have said if she had seen this?' and pulled up his left trouser leg to show a much worse injury.

At the age of eighty, George went missing for one day. Neither his son and daughter-in-law nor his daughters had any idea where he might be. Late in the evening he returned home much satisfied with his day: he had taken a lady for a day out at Blackpool.

Another incident in George's later years shows his love of scoring points during an argument. A young insurance salesman called at the house to talk to George with the aim of persuading him to take out a policy to cover funeral costs. George listened quietly while the insurance agent went through every detail of the insurance policy, stressing all the benefits for everyone and covering every point he could think of, as George said nothing. At last, when the man had no more to say, George said 'Tell me, young man, have you ever seen anybody left on t'top?'

'No,' said the young man.

'Well then,' said George, 'I don't need your insurance.'

When George died he was buried in a grave which had already been used and there was little room to lower the coffin. Those present had never seen anyone left so near the top.

George died peacefully at home at the age of eighty-five. The last word he spoke was 'Ethel', the daughter who had died before him, so contributing to the widely held belief that someone from 'the other side' comes to help or welcome the dying.

His gravestone was a simple, semi-circular block of Bramley Fall stone, at his own request, bearing just the letters *G-R / B* , his business trademark.

GEORGE'S CHILDREN

The Daughters

JANE

George and Elizabeth's ten children were so spread out in age that some had little significant association with others. The eldest, Jane, had married and moved away from Bramley before the youngest children were born. It is known that she had the usual basic education as a child and she had worked for some years, before her marriage, in a local mill as a worsted weaver. Whatever contact she kept with the rest of the family did not seem to have made a great impression on her younger sisters and brothers, as in later years, she almost seemed to have been forgotten. When they reminisced, it was often '... oh, and I think Jane might have been there as well.' There was some contact, however, as it was known that she had three children and that she died before George.

EDITH

In contrast with Jane, Edith, who was only two years younger, was a very prominent and positive member of the family group. She too, after working as a worsted weaver, married and did not live in Bramley but, living at a distance of only two or three miles away, she remained very much interested and involved with Bramley matters. Her husband, Edward Ibbotson, became a popular member of the family and shared his wife's interest in attending Bramley events. They had four children, three boys and a girl. Edith's young brothers were very amused to think that they were uncles to nephews who were older than them. One of Edith's sons went to America 'to Hollywood – to be a film star'. There was no report of success.

FOUR SISTERS. Left to right: Maude, Kate, Edith, Lillie in mid-1930s fashions.

Maude and Lillie

These two sisters must be considered together. With only about two years between them in age they were close companions for the whole of their lives, although they were quite different in character. Like all George's children they attended the local National School and attended Sunday school and church regularly. At school they were keen pupils and also enjoyed playing hockey. Additionally they both had the usual household jobs. One important job that they and the other children had to do, when young, was to get water from the town well when there was no efficient system of piped water. In very severe frosts the water in the town well froze, and at such times, the water had to be obtained from a spring in the valley known locally as Jacob's Well, which did not freeze. The return journey of almost half a mile mostly uphill was the part they remembered most clearly.

On leaving school, they both went to work in a local mill as worsted weavers. Lillie spent her entire working life in this mill. They also, when the seasonal rhubarb required extra hands, put all their 'spare' time into the family business.

Despite their working hours and other tasks, Maude and Lillie, and all their sisters, took every opportunity to enjoy what social functions there were. For the more formal occasions special preparations were made, not only with regards to suitable clothing – which simply meant wearing one's best – but applying the nearest they could get to facial cosmetics. There were few cosmetic preparations available in Bramley and they could not afford what would have been available in Leeds. They did what other Bramley young ladies did: a touch of beetroot on the cheeks and an application of flour to serve instead of face powder.

TYPICAL BRAMLEY LADIES c. 1920. Maude and Lillie at the end of the yard (photographed by Ilbert).

They got on well together even though they had very different temperaments. Maude was placid, tolerant and unhurried. At home she was sometimes referred to as 'Miss Easiful', and she was not known for doing more than had to be done, although competent and well organised in whatever she did. By contrast, Lillie was brisk, forthright, authoritative and outgoing. Neither had any great romance, and they were quite content with the life they lived. Being Rileys of Bramley mattered to them and they did all they were able to do for the family and for Bramley, most of their activity being directed towards the church and the Conservative Club.

The recently built new church of St Peter, erected only a few years before they were born, was important to them, not only because it was the most impressive building in Bramley but because their family had contributed towards the cost, even if they misunderstood just what the contribution had been. When young, most of George's family had a church-going pattern of 8 a.m. Holy Communion, 10.30 a.m. Matins, 2 p.m. Sunday School, and 6.30 p.m. Evensong. Lillie was rather proud of this – she continued to attend services regularly every week until old age – but Maude the realist said 'Well, there was nothing else to do!'

Years later when encouraging a young niece who had not previously attended Evensong to sit with her, Lillie said 'The Riley's pew is the second from the front on the side where the Vicar sits. We don't sit in the front pew because it would look as though we were putting ourselves forward to be noticed.'

To which Maude added with a slight smile: 'But no one ever comes to sit in the front pew!'

Maude, although very interested in all that concerned the church, did not, from the time of her father's old age, continue to attend church every week. After quite a long interval she went to one service and a woman in the pew behind collapsed and died there. It was a long time before Maude went to church again.

Much earlier than the events mentioned above, George had moved into a larger stone-built house, Prospect Cottage, and through marriages, work commitments, and deaths there ceased to be a family home in the old sense. Ilbert, and after his marriage, his wife, lived with George. Maude and Lillie moved into a small one-storey two-roomed cottage adjoining George's house. The two rooms in this cottage were a kitchen and a bedroom. The bedroom had an early type of sofa bed so that when required the room could serve as a sitting room. There was no bathroom and the toilet was outdoors across the yard. The Yorkist Range met most needs of heating and cooking.

All George's daughters were seriously interested in his political work, especially where it concerned Bramley. Both Maude and Lillie in particular were active at election times, went to political meetings and were prominent figures in the social activities centred on the Conservative Club.

Lillie enjoyed political talks and debates, and Maude was

for quite a number of years the President of the Bramley branch of the Primrose League. It was the custom for a small celebration tea party to be arranged when a member reached the age of seventy, but Maude tried never to reveal her age (she had at home demonstrated the ability to do high kicks when admitting to being 'turned sixty') so even Primrose League members who had more or less grown up with her were not quite sure of her exact age. At last, a deputation shyly said 'We know it must be about time to celebrate your seventieth birthday. When would you like us to hold the tea party?' Maude graciously gave them a date, although she never ceased to be vastly amused that they had missed the proper date by about four or five years.

A quieter source of pleasure for these two sisters was the Bramley countryside. Having been used, for so many years, to walking a lot out of necessity, they continued to walk for pleasure. Bramley Fall Woods offered the favourite walks at most times of the year: early spring to gather catkins and pussy willow for decoration, around May time when the bluebells covered the ground, leafy shade in summer, and colours in the autumn. At any time of the year these walks were used to provide not only exercise and peaceful interludes but also various utilitarian purposes. There were nettles for nettle beer, elderflowers and elderberries for cordial and wine, blackberries for pies and jam, and plenty of firewood to be gathered. In addition there were good viewpoints for a panorama of a stretch of the Aire valley. When going on these walks Maude usually took her 'dog-knorper' – a combination of walking stick and club for beating off any fierce dogs. Years earlier she had seen her Pekinese dog savaged by a larger dog and seriously hurt so that it had to be put down, so her wariness about stray dogs was understandable.

Between them, Maude and Lillie had quite a store of traditional cures for various ailments and natural products for household purposes. A popular remedy for respiratory tract infections was a gently warmed mixture of honey, butter, and vinegar, or the juice resulting from brown sugar applied to a sliced turnip. They made their own cottage cheese, and of course got fresh vegetables from the market garden.

In old age, they were looked after for a while by a niece, then when Maude died Lillie lived in a retirement home (in Bramley, of course) where she was inclined to bore the other residents by constantly airing her father's achievements and opinions.

ETHEL, a fashionable Bramley lady.

Ethel

Ethel had no specially close companion among her sisters. The general impression is that she was self-sufficient and home-loving. There was even a slight suspicion that if George could be said to have a favourite daughter it might have been Ethel. Her death earlier than her brothers and sisters was not treated as anything demanding special explanation.

Kate

The early years of Kate's life were so much like those of her sisters that repetition would be tedious. The youngest of the girls, she was keen to appear as grown-up as her sisters, but also being nearer in age to brothers she shared some of their games. She was lively, outgoing and energetic, in personality and attitudes much like Lillie but with a very 'comfortable' sense of humour. When she married it was into a well-known Bramley family and she continued to live locally. There were three children of this marriage: a boy and two girls.

WEDDING GROUP – Kate's elder daughter, c. 1935. The young bridesmaid on the left is the author!

BLUEBELL TIME IN BRAMLEY FALL

'It isn't in the guide book,' a lady chanced to say,
'But Bramley Fall is lovely, 'tis a vale of bluebells gay!'
'A bluebell vale at Bramley? Where is it? Tell us pray,
For surely such a sight is good, on a glorious day in May!
So we have followed the directions, and words were
   put to flight
For the Fall Woods, clothed in bluebells, were indeed a
   wondrous sight,
Neath the beeches, ash and oak trees, and sycamores so
   green,
'Twas the greatest sea of bluebells, that we had ever seen.

They made a lovely carpet, as far as our eyes could see
Shimmering 'midst the bracken, waving 'neath the trees
Ringing out their message, with fragrance, on the air,
'Cheerio, look around you, there's beauty everywhere.'

So, if 'fed up with Bramley', and you call it dull and grey,
Just take a walk down Bramley Fall, on any pleasant day,
But especially is it beautiful, in bluebell time each year,
And, once seen, 'twill be remembered, when days are
   dark and drear.

*Hilda M Myers – well known to George's daughters and all
'Old' Bramley. Owner of the Fent Shop.*

The Sons

Louis

The third of George's children was his oldest son, Louis. Louis had a family nickname: he was usually referred to by his brothers and sisters as 'Luppy'. No explanation was given as to how this nickname came about, but it may have originated in a childish attempt to pronounce his real name.

At school he was probably a conscientious pupil, as the one tiny sample of his handwriting still in existence shows neatly executed copperplate writing. Little was ever said about either his schooldays or his life in the following years. On leaving school he was employed in the shoe trade. Bramley had for a long time had a flourishing leather trade; tanning, boots and shoes of a good reputation were produced by cottage industry and later by larger businesses. Apprentices often lived in the home of the master shoemaker, and even if Louis did not do this, he would spend long working hours away from home.

After his working life Louis became a somewhat solitary figure, living alone in a small stone cottage and having little direct contact with his brothers or sisters even though some of them lived within half a mile of his cottage. He was far from being unusual in not wanting much social contact and preferring to live his life in his own way. One of his immediate neighbours in the small terrace of cottages was an extreme example of this. Each of the cottages had a strip of garden in front, and at the far end of the gardens away from the road were the outside toilets. The toilets were shielded from the road by a short length of wall but the open ends allowed some view of the toilet cubicles to passers-by going up or down the road. One old lady, Louis's neighbour, had a habit of going to the toilet and leaving the toilet door wide open because 'she liked a bit of fresh air.' Sometimes she would stay there for a time, singing happily if tunelessly. No one made any protest.

One unhappy incident in Louis's life occurred in these later years. He had a dog for company and took good care of it, but when it was old and ill he tried to prevent its suffering by killing it himself, by either strangling or hanging. This was reported and he was charged with cruelty to the animal and fined.

Near the end of his life Louis nominally became a Roman Catholic. His brothers and sisters had no doubt that this was because the local Roman Catholic church had a social programme by which pensioners were given financial or other help, and Louis would rather accept help from strangers than from his family, to keep up a pretence that he could manage on his own.

FRED

Fred's early years with the family were unremarkable. He did not have a really close attachment to any of his brothers, but he was positively enough a member of the group to have a nickname. He was known as 'Botolph', without there being any clear reason why that name was given.

Unfortunately there is no family information about how he passed his time when young. At some point it must have been obvious that he had a good ear because he spent his adult life as an organ tuner. Bramley had both a firm of organ builders and one of organ pipe makers, so there would be no difficulty in learning his craft. He went on to work independently, able to negotiate his own contracts. His organ tuning engagements took him to many places throughout Great Britain and he was therefore not greatly involved with Bramley public or social life.

His home when he was in Bramley was a rather unkempt looking building standing on its own among fields far away from many other houses. He lived alone there. His sisters Maude and Lillie gave him some support and even if they could not be said to 'mother' him they were there when he wished to talk and they also provided occasional meals. They, not being great travellers, liked to hear about the places he visited, although to some extent this was an excuse to try to help him over his problem with drink. Living alone at home, travelling alone, often working alone, and staying in bed and breakfast accommodation when working away, Fred's main relaxation was with the companionship he found in public houses. Later there were solitary drinking bouts.

He did not let this affect his work. In negotiating his own contracts he stipulated that he could take a few days off when he wished, which gave him time to recover from too heavy a drinking session. Of his many organ tuning jobs the one which probably gave him the most satisfaction was working on the organ of the newly built Anglican Cathedral at Liverpool.

Ilbert

George and Elizabeth had more discussion over the name of their ninth child than all the rest put together. George, with his great interest in Bramley, which included its history, wanted this son to be named Ilbert de Laci after an early owner of the land on which Bramley developed and Kirkstall Abbey was built. Elizabeth thought this was unsuitable (perhaps too pretentious?) and wanted something plainer. The compromise was just Ilbert.

Problems did not end there; the next one arose when the birth was registered. Elizabeth suddenly realised that when only the initial I was used with Riley it could also stand for Isaac, and she insisted that she was not having her son mistaken for the black sheep of the family, so the name must be altered: an 'H' could be added at the beginning. The registrar carefully explained that the birth certificate was a very important legal document and could not be changed. Elizabeth would not give way; it must be changed.

The registrar conceded defeat and with his own hand crossed out the capital I and wrote above it 'Hi'. The baby was christened Ilbert as originally planned. In later years when a birth certificate had to be shown Ilbert had the problem of explaining why he signed his name *I* Riley when according to the birth certificate it should be *H*!

ILBERT, c. 1920. A studio photograph taken about the time of his engagement to Vera.

A small incident when Ilbert was about two years old shows that there were (circa 1890) still uneducated, simple people to be found in Bramley. Elizabeth was making bread and gave young Ilbert a small lump of dough to eat. He ran outside on the rough, unsurfaced road and fell. The dough came out of his mouth onto the ground, and a woman seeing this ran over to him and tried to force the dough back into his mouth. She shrieked out 'Poor bairn! His innards are coming out! He's losing his innards!' His mother was less worried.

Another very minor mishap occurred when Ilbert was about seven years old. He had a boil on one leg, and his mother was applying a homemade medication on a cloth heated at the coal fire. Ilbert very loudly declared that it was too hot, and was sharply told to be quiet and not make a fuss about something that was being done to help him. When the cloth was removed from his leg a hot ember from the fire had been caught up in it and had been pressed against the sore point.

He had a happy childhood and did very well at school. Before he left school at the age of twelve, Ilbert, in one year in open competition with others of his age and older, won every subject prize except Handwriting.

Before and after leaving school he did of course have plenty of time to join friends in a variety of activities. They roamed freely through the area, enjoying the woods, the canal, the various small becks, and getting to know the neighbouring villages as well as every part of Bramley. There were occasional outbursts of high spirits in the group. From time to time quite a large group of boys would rush madly down the shopping area of Town Street wreaking havoc by overturning the displays of goods outside many shops. A favourite target was the hardware shop where so many articles made a lot of noise when knocked down. The boys could disappear in a few moments down ginnels, yards and passageways, so that few were ever caught.

In Ilbert's time another popular 'nuisance' game for a group was to go out towards the local railway line between Bramley and Pudsey when a train was due and throw stones at the engine. It was satisfying to hear the clang as the stones hit the engine, but the real fun came when the engine driver, known to have a quick temper, would stop the train, get down from the cab, and chase them across the fields – he never caught anyone.

Ilbert and his younger brother Galen did many things together, whether fighting or playing with each other. Once, knowing that their parents liked them to look smart, they thought that their smart dark best suits with Eton-style collars and 'bum-starver' jackets were let down by their somewhat unruly hair. So, finding a tin of clear varnish they carefully varnished each other's hair. They found out painfully that their parents were not pleased.

ILBERT (back row, second from left), c. 1904, with a Church Lads' Brigade sports group.

As a teenager Ilbert worked long hours in the family's business, and his interests after work were purposeful and pursued seriously. He was a capable musician, and as a member of the Church Lads' Brigade he played several instruments; the flute remained a favourite. He also played the piano and the organ. He was given no favours for learning the organ although his father was a churchwarden and an uncle was the Verger. Told that he could practise on the church organ for an hour, Ilbert would find his uncle standing near him as the hour drew to a close, watch in hand, saying 'Thou seest what time it is, lad.'

'Yes, uncle,' Ilbert would reply and immediately finish playing. In due course he became a church organist and a choirmaster. He was a good gymnast and swimmer and played in sports teams with the Church Lads' Brigade. He also took advantage of public lectures, readings and discussions, and read widely.

At the beginning of the Great War in 1914 Ilbert went to enlist in the army, but was told that agricultural work was as important.

When organist and choirmaster at a church in Armley he met Vera Jane Denison and married her in 1922.

ILBERT AND VERA'S WEDDING, 1922. Back row left: George and Galen (best man).

The couple lived with George in Prospect Cottage, and three children, two boys and a girl, were born there. Ilbert was now running the market garden in place of George.

It was a difficult time for making a living from market gardening, but Ilbert was always ready to accept challenges. There was a particularly serious one shortly after George's death. Severe weather in a bad winter had almost destroyed the commercial greenhouse which was necessary for the crops of tomatoes and chrysanthemums which were the main money crops in summer and autumn. The greenhouse was a large A-shaped wooden frame on a low brick supporting wall, and gale force winds had not only moved the frame to shatter much of the glass, but had forced the frame partly off the brick supporting wall. Ilbert, who was very strong, picked up a large piece of timber, and standing inside the greenhouse and holding this beam much in the manner of 'tossing the caber' gently placed it against the central beam of the greenhouse. Then very slowly and smoothly eased up the whole frame and inch by inch he moved the whole structure back into place on the brick support. He was well aware that the slightest slip or jarring movement could cause the remaining glass to fall with very serious consequences for himself, but he had the strength of nerve as well as of body, and accomplished what he had determined to do.

In the 1920s and '30s market gardening and rhubarb growing in particular did not bring in as much money as in the previous century. Ilbert concentrated on quality products, which continued to sell, and at the rhubarb growers' annual show held each February he usually won prizes, even the Rose Bowl! Evidence of the quality of his rhubarb is testified in a letter from a Cambridgeshire wholesaler in 1944.

Dear Sir

Many thanks for the box of marvellous rhubarb, we have never seen anything like it, all our men are astounded, and we can assure you it is greatly appreciated. We have divided it round the best we could, and all who have shared wish us to convey their very best thanks, and also to congratulate you on being able to produce such fine quality rhubarb, you must certainly be a past master at this work.

Wishing you every success

p.p.———
(Secretary)

It was not only commercial contacts who got his best products. Perhaps because of his knowledge of his father's and grandfather's early years, or just because it was his nature, Ilbert had a lot of sympathy for people who had to struggle to make ends meet. Frequently when sending small deliveries to local people, Ilbert would put in some extra peas, potatoes and so on, or providing a huge cabbage or cauliflower would say 'That costs... No, she hasn't much money. Tell her it costs a penny.' He did not wish to make money out of people who had little to live on at any time, but there were times when he had little enough money himself. In 1945 he sent *twenty bags* (or sacks) of top grade cabbages to Leeds market, and received only £4 10s.

During the years of the Second World War Ilbert was running the business without help and working very long hours. He was asked to be the street Air Raid Warden for the area in which he lived, but he slept so soundly that he never heard the air raid siren and had to be woken up to be told of the air raid warning. Fortunately Bramley, and Leeds had few such alarms and little significant bomb damage. One of the few occasions when Ilbert was really angry was when one of the very few bombs to fall on the Bramley area fell on his potato crop. It was not being bombed that made him angry - it was that people from round about came to pick up and take away the potatoes thrown up by the explosion without thinking how it affected his livelihood although they would not have taken the potatoes in normal circumstances.

Only after his death did anyone but his wife know that for many years as well as providing for his own family he had been paying off a large mortgage left by his father and paying the rent for Maude and Lillie's cottage.

He was a man of great ability and admirable character who spent his life working for the good of others.

GALEN

The youngest of George's ten children was a close companion to Ilbert, and little can be said about his early years which has not already been indicated. Of a slighter build and not quite as clever as Ilbert, he still shared all or most of the same activities as a child and as a young man. As boys they fought each other, laughed together, and supported each other whenever circumstances required it. On the business side, Galen's main interest was the ordinary market gardening and he played a significant part in securing new markets for the vegetables and rhubarb. In the course of this he met Gladys, married her and went to live in Leicester where he bought a shop and became a greengrocer. He returned to Bramley to be best man at Ilbert's wedding. Little was heard of him, except perhaps by Ilbert, but the main incident in the rest of his life is best told in his own words in a letter to Ilbert dated September 22 1927:

Dear Ilbert,

Accept my most sincere gratitude for the money and thoughts in your letters, the same being the only true feelings I have had shown to me since Sunday, and for which I return (and have done many times during my solitude) a true brother's hand-grip, also I know Gladys can see this at the present time. I regret greatly you will not be with me this afternoon the time of the funeral, although I shall still feel your handclasp throughout the sad occasion. As you know, I had nursed Gladys day and night for the last twelve months, during that time her case was in the hands of two specialists and two doctors.

But it was not to be, as they cried off about March, since then I took the job on, but knew we were losing all the time as the cancer which was in the hinge of the right jaw bone had got firm hold of the cheek, right eye, and down the neck. The torture she went through is now indescribable. I often found her knelt down praying to be taken.

When she felt all right she would go down to her mother's occasionally for tea, but this little pleasure was to be denied her, as her sisters and brothers told her mother they did not want to have their tea with her at the table. So poor Glad was an outcast, so I told Glad if she wasn't to go, I wasn't going, and consoled her with 'Bah! The same unthinking crowd!' Well, this went on until the 5th of this month when her mother took it on her to write to Dr Mackerel the specialist, and he wrote her back saying it was a sad case, as they would not have her back at the Royal Infirmary, and the cost of a private one would be about 5 to 6 guineas a week, and there was only one place for her, the North Evington Infirmary, which is the Workhouse Infirmary and that he would like to see me. I went and took Glad with me on September 8th. Mackerel examined her, then took me in the other room and told me the same as he said in the letter, so I asked him what time she had left on this earth, two weeks, two months, or how long, as, if it wasn't for long I was going to stick to her; this he could not say. However, her own people wouldn't have her, and I was done up all ways, having sold the shop, which when nearly all debts were paid left me with £3, I still owe £20 to a money lender, Glad's mother £60, Glad's sister £10, but these two latter leave it to me as I can't fall out with them yet as the funeral will cost £15-0-0, you understand my reasons.

Well, to get on with it, I thought if they could let her go to the WH Infirmary I could, although it is not like Bramley, it being in the country about 3 miles from the WH proper so it wasn't so bad. Well, I saw the Officer on Saturday September 10th, when he asked where I was working and how much wage. Of course, I said out of work; any insurance? None. Well, they fetched her on

Monday the 12th, sent me a sick notice on Tuesday entitling me to visit her daily between 8 a.m. and 9.30 p.m.. I did so until Saturday last when her mother and sister thought they would go. They gave me their report at night and they had found her lively, walking out with them to the corridor. Well, Sunday morning came and also a telegram to me at 10 o'clock, Glad seriously ill, go immediately. I got there at 10.45 but poor Glad was unconscious. I stayed until 12.15 when I saw the Sister, and asked if she thought Glad would be right until after dinner when I would come back, as they (nurses) were getting other patients' dinners ready in the ward. She said yes she thought so, so I left. Went back at 2.30 but Glad had gone, never regaining consciousness. They laid her out and I stayed about 10 minutes with her. I came away, carrying her handbag and the magazines I had taken her, walking down the long drive like one in a dream, not a soul anywhere, not a bird singing, now I realized I was left alone. I sincerely hope you have not that walk to go; if I could only have met you.

Well, I went on Monday morning for the certificate but the doctor wanted to see me, he wanted my permission for a post-mortem. I gave it and he talked with me for half an hour, saying Glad was the finest character he had met during his 30 years experience. I went on Wednesday and saw him and he said that they had done it and that she had died a beautiful death as the cancer had gripped one part of the brain and another part was penetrating the spinal column at the neck, which he said would be a painless, peaceful and beautiful death. So you have it now, Ilbert, briefly, but I hope to tell you more later. So, God bless you and yours.

Your grateful brother,

Galen

There was little further contact between Galen and his brothers and sisters, even including Ilbert. After George's funeral in 1931 little more was heard from Galen. In 1949 he visited Bramley for the last time, to attend Ilbert's funeral.

AN ODE TO BRAMLEY TOWN STREET

Why did they pull down old Bramley Town Street?
We'll never get over t'shock.
Why did they pull down Town Street
On'y to build some new shops?
They said it were to give it a face-lift
It were said they would widen t'road.
But they on'y did nowt but damage
They should heve left place alone.
When you think on t'folk that 'av lived there
When you think on t'good times they've had
When you think, they must 'av been happy
Cos they'd Carnival, Feast an' t'Brass Band.
Now it's too late to do owt about it
But at least we can look back on t'past
And try to remember what happened
And how it all came to pass.
Tha's many a one has good memories
And there's many a one has some sad
But you try to look on t'place wi' nostalgia
And you think of a place that wer'nt bad.
So now, there's things we put up wi'
Though things'll nivver be t'same
For ther's that new shopping centre
All modern and posh and clean
Wi' Morrisons, Co-op and Boots,
Ther's Sea Land Food and Houghs,
But they'll nivver beat old Bramley Town Street
With its one-mile long row of shops.

It were stone-built and had character,
It had yards with old cobble stoned streets
Built higgledy-piggledy, with plenty of people to meet.
You could walk all on t'owd ginnels
You could go through 'Tusky Fields' and roam.
In fact, it were more like a village,
A grand place you called home.
There went Lido, Clifton, and tramcars
And plenty of pubs as well
Such as *Cardigan Arms*, *New Inn*, *Star and Garter*,
Not forgetting t'old school, Bramley National.
Though most of it's gone now, you still see it
There in t'minds eye,
The memories of old Bramley Town Street,
The spirit that nivver will die.

Mabel Birley

EPILOGUE

In the second half of the twentieth century all the Rileys who were directly descended from George gradually left Bramley: some died, some removed to neighbouring 'townships' within the Leeds area, and others moved much further away. No doubt there are still people in Bramley who are descendants of the wider family, even if not of the same surname through marriages, but they are not in evidence as a 'family'.

Perhaps a little of the old feeling for Bramley is still to be found in present residents. About 1980, a curate new to the parish was trying to get to know a small group of youths on one of the housing estates; 'What's it like, living in Leeds?' he asked them.

They gazed at him blankly, then one said: 'Don't knaw, we're Bramley.'

Floreat Brameleia!